T0034128

ARCHAIC
SMILE

ARCHAIC SMILE

FARRAR STRAUS GIROUX / NEW YORK

A. E. STALLINGS

Farrar, Straus and Giroux
120 Broadway, New York 10271

Some of the poems in this collection previously appeared in the
following publications: *The American Voice*, *Atlanta Review*, *Beloit Poetry
Journal*, *The Classical Outlook*, *ELF: Electric Literary Forum*, *Edge City
Review*, *Five Points*, *The Formalist*, *The Lyric*, *Oxford American*, and *Poetry*.

Library of Congress Cataloging-in-Publication Data
Names: Stallings, A. E. (Alicia Elsbeth), 1968– author.
Title: Archaic smile : poems / A.E. Stallings.
Description: First paperback edition. | New York : Farrar, Straus and
    Giroux, 2022.
Identifiers: LCCN 2022023785 | ISBN 9780374600723 (paperback)
Subjects: LCSH: Mythology, Classical—Poetry. | LCGFT: Poetry.
Classification: LCC PS3569.T3197 A89 2022 | DDC 811/.54—dc23/eng/
    20220525
LC record available at https://lccn.loc.gov/2022023785

Designed by Crisis

www.fsgbooks.com
www.twitter.com/fsgbooks
www.facebook.com/fsgbooks

1 3 5 7 9 10 8 6 4 2

CONTENTS

I

UNDERWORLD

A POSTCARD FROM GREECE

Hatched from sleep, as we slipped out of orbit
Round a clothespin curve new-watered with the rain,
I saw the sea, the sky, as bright as pain,
That outer space through which we were to plummet.
No guardrails hemmed the road, no way to stop it,
The only warning, here and there, a shrine:
Some tended still, some antique and forgotten,
Empty of oil, but all were consecrated
To those who lost their wild race with the road
And sliced the tedious sea once, like a knife.
Somehow we struck an olive tree instead.
Our car stopped on the cliff's brow. Suddenly safe,
We clung together, shade to pagan shade,
Surprised by sunlight, air, this afterlife.

HADES WELCOMES HIS BRIDE

Come now, child, adjust your eyes, for sight
Is here a lesser sense. Here you must learn
Directions through your fingertips and feet
And map them in your mind. I think some shapes
Will gradually appear. The pale things twisting
Overhead are mostly roots, although some worms
Arrive here clinging to their dead. Turn here.
Ah. And in this hall will sit our thrones,
And here you shall be queen, my dear, the queen
Of all men ever to be born. No smile?
Well, some solemnity befits a queen.
These thrones I have commissioned to be made
Are unlike any you imagined; they glow
Of deep-black diamonds and lead, subtler
And in better taste than gold, as will suit
Your timid beauty and pale throat. Come now,
Down these winding stairs, the air more still
And dry and easier to breathe. Here is a room
For your diversions. Here I've set a loom
And silk unravelled from the finest shrouds
And dyed the richest, rarest shades of black.
Such pictures you shall weave! Such tapestries!

For you I chose those three thin shadows there,
And they shall be your friends and loyal maids,
And do not fear from them such gossiping
As servants usually are wont. They have
Not mouth nor eyes and cannot thus speak ill
Of you. Come, come. This is the greatest room;
I had it specially made after great thought
So you would feel at home. I had the ceiling
Painted to recall some evening sky—
But without the garish stars and lurid moon.
What? That stark shape crouching in the corner?
Sweet, that is to be our bed. Our bed.
Ah! Your hand is trembling! I fear
There is, as yet, too much pulse in it.

PERSEPHONE WRITES
A LETTER TO HER MOTHER

First—hell is not so far underground—
My hair gets tangled in the roots of trees
& I can just make out the crunch of footsteps,
The pop of acorns falling, or the chime
Of a shovel squaring a fresh grave or turning
Up the tulip bulbs for separation.
Day & night, creatures with no legs
Or too many, journey to hell and back.
Alas, the burrowing animals have dim eyesight.
They are useless for news of the upper world.
They say the light is "loud" (their figures of speech
All come from sound; their hearing is acute).

The dead are just as dull as you would imagine.
They evolve like the burrowing animals—losing their sight.
They may roam abroad sometimes—but just at night—
They can only tell me if there was a moon.
Again and again, moth-like, they are duped
By any beckoning flame—lamps and candles.
They come back startled & singed, sucking their fingers,
Happy the dirt is cool and dense and blind.

They are silly & grateful and don't remember anything.
I have tried to tell them stories, but they cannot attend.
They pester you like children for the wrong details—
How long were his fingernails? Did she wear shoes?
How much did they eat for breakfast? What is snow?
And then they pay no attention to the answers.

My husband, bored with their babbling, neither listens nor
    speaks.
But here there is no fodder for small talk.
The weather is always the same. Nothing happens.
(Though at times I feel the trees, rocking in place
Like grief, clenching the dirt with tortuous toes.)
There is nothing to eat here but raw beets & turnips.
There is nothing to drink but mud-filtered rain.
Of course, no one goes hungry or toils, however many—
(The dead breed like the bulbs of daffodils—
Without sex or seed—all underground—
Yet no race has such increase. Worse than insects!)

I miss you and think about you often.
Please send flowers. I am forgetting them.
If I yank them down by the roots, they lose their petals
And smell of compost. Though I try to describe
Their color and fragrance, no one here believes me.
They think they are the same thing as mushrooms.

Yet no dog is so loyal as the dead,
Who have no wives or children and no lives,
No motives, secret or bare, to disobey.
Plus, my husband is a kind, kind master;
He asks nothing of us, nothing, nothing at all—
Thus fall changes to winter, winter to fall,
While we learn idleness, a difficult lesson.

He does not understand why I write letters.
He says that you will never get them. True—
Mulched-leaf paper sticks together, then rots;
No ink but blood, and it turns brown like the leaves.
He found my stash of letters, for I had hid it,
Thinking he'd be angry. But he never angers.
He took my hands in his hands, my shredded fingers
Which I have sliced for ink, thin paper cuts.
My effort is futile, he says, and doesn't forbid it.

FROM WHOSE BOURN NO TRAVELLER

Death, the deportation officer,
Has seen your papers and has found them wanting.
Discrepancies in why you came to visit:
Pleasure, you said, then business. Which is it?
Your intentions are not clear, but he suspects
That you are trying to stay here forever.

Your claim, that you cannot be replaced,
Holds no water. Others can pick the tomatoes,
Smell the gardenia at sunset, stroke the cat,
Watch over your lover deep in a pillow of dreams.

You protest—so long ago, I cannot remember
Anything about where I came from. Not even the language.
They say but for dogs and buzzards the village is empty.
They say, there is no work. There is nothing to eat.
No phone, no way even to send a letter
To the girl I want to marry, waiting at home.

Your case is closed, he says, stamping your folder.
The others waiting in the holding cell
Assure you that the language will come back,
An uninflected tongue, without number or gender,
In which *hello*'s the same word as *goodbye*.

EURYDICE REVEALS HER STRENGTH

Dying is the easy part.
As you still live, my dear, why did you come?
You should learn an easing of the heart
As I have, now, for truly some

Prefer this clarity of mind, this death
Of all the body's imperious demands:
That constant interruption of the breath,
That fever-greed of eyes and hands

To digest your beauty whole.
You strike a tune upon a string:
They say that it is beautiful.
You sing to me, you sing, you sing.

I think, how do the living hear?
But I remember now, that it was just
A quiver in the membrane of the ear,
And love, a complicated lust.

And I remember now, as in a book,
How you pushed me down upon the grass and stones,
Crushed me with your kisses and your hands and took
What there is to give of emptiness, and moans.

We strained to be one strange new beast enmeshed,
And this is what we strained against, this death,
And clawed as if to peel away the flesh,
Crawled safe inside another's hollowness,

Because we feared this calm of being dead.
I say this. You abhor my logic, and you shiver,
Thinking I may as well be just some severed head
Floating down a cool, forgetful river,

Slipping down the shadows, green and black,
Singing to myself, not looking back.

EURYDICE'S FOOTNOTE

... a single Hellenistic poem, on which Virgil
and Ovid drew freely ... made a vitally important
change by turning the recovery of Eurydice,
whether complete or temporary, into a tragic loss.
—C. M. Bowra, *The Classical Quarterly*, 1952

Love, then, always was a matter of revision
As reality, to poet or to politician
Is but the first rough draft of history or legend.
So your artist's eye, a sharp and perfect prism,
Refracts discrete components of a beauty
To fix them in some still more perfect order.
(I say this on the other side of order
Where things can be re-invented no longer.)

Still I recall, at times, the critical moment
When nothing was so difficult as you had wanted,
And knowing my love would grow back for you like any crop,
You turned your head, an inhospitable, cold planet
(Your eyes—flash, flash, like sickles)—
How the sun grew far away again and small
As a red eye at the telescope's far tapering.
Life proved fickle as any lover.

I still imagine your explanation, were it to come,
As in some catalogued and hard-bound learned journal
Speaking with 100 iron tongues of respected criticism:

Disappointment in the end was more aesthetic
Than any merely felicitous resolution.

HOW THE DEMONS WERE ASSIMILATED
& BECAME PRODUCTIVE CITIZENS

The demons were more beautiful than the angels.
They had no qualms about plastic surgery.
They took to wearing black: didn't show dirt
In the city like Innocence, which anyway
Couldn't be worn between Labor Day and Easter.
They tired of grudging angels their gilded hair
& had theirs done. Their complexions were so pale
The blond looked natural, only more so.
They shrunk their wings into fashionable tattoos
So cashmere suits draped better from their shoulders.
Elocution lessons turned hisses to lisps.

The demons converted. They became Episcopalian,
Name-dropped high-ups in the Company of Heaven.
As for Evil, it became too much trouble:
The demons started to shirk the menial jobs
Which, like good deeds, took one among the poor,
And bruised the manicure of rose-petal nails.
They preferred to stand by & watch Evil happen,
Or offended by odors & noise, even turned away.

They had become so beautiful, even the angels
(Who never looked in mirrors to comb their hair,
Afraid to be called vain, & never bought clothes
Since the old ones didn't wear out, just got shabby)
Left the lovely demons to languish, dropping all charges
On the spoiled creatures. They were that good.

THE DOGDOM OF THE DEAD

There is no dog so loyal as the Dead,
Always with you, trotting along at your heels,
Or snoring lightly and taking up most of the bed,
Their paw pads twitching and their tails a-wag.

For even in your slumber, they still tag,
Dawdling behind and charging ahead,
Sniffing a memory out like a fleeting rabbit,
But always losing the scent when it crosses the Styx.

They are creatures of habit and cannot learn new tricks.
But what you would throw away, they fetch back for you,
A game they never tire of, and what you would keep,
They bury in the ground, a hoard of bones.

If you try to sneak off without them, they sound such moans—
Wind skinning itself in the trees, the boo-hoo of trains—
And then come bounding behind you, faithful as shadows.
You will come to prefer them, dumb and dogged, forgiving,

For the Living, like cats, insinuate into your arms,
And when they've licked everything clean, dictated their terms,
They stray back into the moonlight and other kitchens,
Ungrateful creatures with their own lives.

ALL HALLOWS

The thin hands of the trees
Blow away, waving goodbye.

Haunted with similes
Is the house of memory—

The one who has departed,
The one who left you alone.

The bulbs are in their bed
Feeding on their meal of bone.

The jack-o'-lanterns bear
Brief, vegetable witness

As ghosts tap at the door
Still hungering after sweetness.

II

A

BESTIARY

CARDINAL NUMBERS

Mrs. Cardinal is dead:
All that remains—a beak of red,
And, fanned across the pavement slab,
Feathers, drab.

Remember how we saw her mate
In the magnolia tree of late,
Glowing, in the faded hour,
A scarlet flower,

And knew, from his nagging sound,
His wife foraged on the ground,
As camouflaged, as he (to us)
Conspicuous?

One of us remarked, with laughter,
It was her safety he looked after,
On the watch, from where he sat,
For dog or cat

(For being lately married we
Thought we had the monopoly,

Nor guessed a bird so glorious
Uxorious).

Of course, the reason that birds flocked
To us: we kept the feeder stocked.
And there are cats (why mince words)
Where there are birds.

A possum came when dusk was grey,
And so tidied the corpse away,
While Mr. Cardinal at dawn
Carried on,

As if to say, he doesn't blame us,
Our hospitality is famous.
If other birds still want to visit,
Whose fault is it?

WORDS OF PREY

we see a large bird of prey in downtown Savannah catch a squirrel

Eagle-struck, we freeze, in all our lives
Never so close as here in the city. Clandestine,
He pulls, long as magic handkerchieves
Tied corner to corner, the squirrel's bright intestine.

We note how impossibly long our insides are,
How larger than our skin. We cannot go.
We are like rabbits pinned by his orange stare
To the comforting earth, and keep our bodies low.

Gripping the twig-thin line between comic and tragic,
Another squirrel looks on, perhaps in grief,
But likelier in safety, heart-beat blunt,

Calmed by this, our shared, natural logic:
How we all look on disaster, with relief,
Thinking, while it feeds it does not hunt.

WATCHING THE VULTURE
AT THE ROAD KILL

You know Death by his leisure—take
The time we saw the vulture make
His slow, hot-air-balloon descent
To a possum smashed beside the pavement.
We stopped the car to watch. Too close.
He bounced his moon-walk bounce and rose
With a shrug up to the kudzu sleeve
Of a pine, to wait for us to leave.
What else can afford to linger?
The eagle has his trigger-finger,
Quails and doves their shell-shocked nerves—
There is no peace but scavengers.

WHY THE SAYING IS
"AS THE CROW FLIES"

Because the buzzard skirts around
The subject, tactful and profound,
Because there is no one can follow
The insect zigzag of the swallow
Among the wings of dusk, because
The hawk is so precipitous,
Because the owl makes no noise
Robbing the rabbit of her voice,
Because the doves would rather be
Safe on the ground, the bourgeoisie,
Grey-suited, plump and gossiping,
And mockingbirds would rather sing
Upon a twig a half a dozen
Stolen tunes, but Raven's cousin
Alone will fly both straight and stark
His course, one feather with the dark.

LISTENING TO THE MONKEYS OF THE NEARBY YERKES REGIONAL PRIMATE RESEARCH CENTER

Humidity has made them homesick,
This thick, cicada-d Georgia June.
The heat is ancient and nostalgic,
Familiar is the doubling moon.

Upon my stoop I hear their calling,
Their long, lugubrious ululations,
In languages, rising, falling,
Of a thousand monkey nations.

The night is shallowed-out with lamp-gloss,
That streets may rise like tricky rivers
Raccoons think they can ford across
To join their families or lovers;

Or possums, with their human feet,
Who also cross, and see as stars
The kind lights swooping down to greet
Them from the swift, oncoming cars.

The night is hollowed-out with fear—
These voices, the bathometer,
This somewhere-past-the-second beer
Helps me but to hardly bear—

I want to call before they stop,
To bridge our two captivities,
But I would wake my neighbors up
Who frown on such proclivities

Of poets or of indigents
Abusing words or alcohol,
Confusing the experiments,
To ask the meaning of it all . . .

No answer comes, no answer comes—
But owls, air-conditioning, trains,
The silence of opposing thumbs,
Superior and sober brains.

RepRoach

There are times that I reproach
Myself because I loathe the roach,
For I've hymned spider, slug and snail,
Whatever's awkward, ugly, pale,

Whatever's many-legged, at fault,
Whose skin is permeable by salt,
Whatever creatures creep abroad
Unloved by anyone but God.

And yet, somehow, it makes me sick,
How aerodynamic they, and quick:
When porch-light interrupts a knot
Of roaches hatching out some plot,

How they run like rumors scattered
By ersatz friends who lately flattered,
And sleek and shiny, slip from sight
Through the loopholes of the night.

I shrink from nothing else that crawls.
It is their elegance appalls:
Tapping away into the bruise
Of dark like patent leather shoes.

LULLABY FOR INSOMNIACS

The moon is a saucer of milk.
Insomnia is a cat.
Lace curtains—spider silk
Casting a shadow net.

Insomnia jumps on the table
And knocks the knickknacks down
As loud as she is able,
Climbs up the taffeta gown.

The spider keeps her temper
And measures out her bunting.
Insomnia's in the hamper.
Both of them are hunting.

Insomnia and the spider
Are hunting the same moth
Whose wings are brown as cider
And dusty as old cloth.

Who let the moth in the door,
Of liberty bereaved it?
What did it come in for?
The reading lamp deceived it.

For a moth will fly to any
Light larger than the moon,
Whatever is as shiny
As the bowl of a spoon,

And singe its papery wings
Or beat them into ashes
Bumping into things.
It is restless as eyelashes.

The moon spills at the brim.
The glass of water spills.
The spider weaves her scrim.
The sleepless take their pills.

Insomnia, grown fat
On table scraps of the past,
Sits like a ziggurat
And dreams about breakfast.

ELEGY FOR A LOGGERHEAD TURTLE WASHED UP ON A SOUTH CAROLINA BEACH

Mourners, bring your moans and myrtle
To the shipwreck of this turtle,
Barnacled, as dull as sand,
Washed up on Death, that long, dry land,

Less like flesh than huge device,
Save liquefaction of its eyes
And blood's dark broth pooled in its beak
Rusted ajar, as if to speak.

Its engine stopped, it shall not swim
Again in waters green and dim.
Its brains shall spark no more to wish
To seek a mate or jellyfish.

This craft began its journey, oh,
Some seventy-five years ago,
But what of it will reach tomorrow?
Only carapace and sorrow.

Mourners, close your eyes and keen
For this broken time machine
Foundered on the present shore.
It shall not travel anymore.

A LAMENT FOR THE DEAD
PETS OF OUR CHILDHOOD

Even now I dream of rabbits murdered
By loose dogs in the dark, the saved-up voice
Spilt on that last terror, or the springtime
Of lost baby rabbits, grey and blind
As moles, that slipped from birth and from the nest
Into a grey, blind rain, became the mud.
And still I gather up their shapes in dreams,
Those poor, leftover Easter eggs, all grey.

That's how we found out death: the strangled bird
Undone by a toy hung in his cage,
The foundlings that would never last the night
Be it pigeon, crippled snake, the kitten
Whose very fleas forsook it in the morning
While we nursed a hangover of hope.

After the death of pets, dolls lay too still
And wooden in the cradle, sister, after
We learned death: not hell, no ghosts or angels,
But a cold thing in the image of a warm thing,
Limp as sleep without the twitch of dreams.

III

TOUR OF THE LABYRINTH

HOMECOMING

for Ashley and Shelby

It was as if she pulled a thread,
Each time he saw her, that unravelled
All the distance he had travelled
To sleep at home in his own bed,
Or sit together in a room
Spinning yarns of monsters, wars,
Hours counted by the chores.
He loved to watch her at the loom:
The fluent wrists, the liquid motion
Of small tasks not thought about,
The shuttle leaping in and out,
Dolphins sewing the torn ocean.

CONSOLATION FOR TAMAR

on the occasion of her breaking an ancient pot

You know I am no archaeologist, Tamar,
And that to me it is all one dust or another.
Still, it must mean something to survive the weather
Of the Ages—earthquake, flood, and war—

Only to shatter in your very hands.
Perhaps it was gravity, or maybe fated—
Although I wonder if it had not waited
Those years in drawers, aeons in distant lands,

And in your fingers' music, just a little
Was emboldened by your blood, and so forgot
That it was not a rosebud, but a pot,
And, trying to unfold for you, was brittle.

APOLLO TAKES CHARGE OF HIS MUSES

They sat there, nine women, much the same age,
The same poppy-red hair, and similar complexions
Freckling much the same in the summer glare,
The same bright eyes of green melting to blue
Melting to golden brown, they sat there,
Nine women, all of them very quiet, one,
Perhaps, was looking at her nails, one plaited
Her hair in narrow strands, one stared at a stone,
One let fall a mangled flower from her hands,
All nine of them very quiet, and the one who spoke
Said, softly:

"Of course he was very charming, and he smiled,
Introduced himself and said he'd heard good things,
Shook hands all round, greeted us by name,
Assured us it would all be much the same,
Explained his policies, his few minor suggestions
Which we would please observe. He looked forward
To working with us. Wouldn't it be fun? Happy
To answer any questions. Any questions? But
None of us spoke or raised her hand, and questions
There were none; what has poetry to do with reason
Or the sun?"

CRAZY TO HEAR THE TALE AGAIN
(THE FALL OF TROY)

... ferit aurea sidera clamor
—Virgil, *Aeneid* 2.488

The stars were golden! Golden as the fire—
We had seen nothing like it, ah, but then
Such things that night, we'll not see such again.
But stars, we'd thought, were purer, somehow: higher—

And yet it seemed a blush that turned them gold.
What once was chill alike to joy or harm
That one strange night seemed somehow to grow warm
And dashed the hopes long cherished by the Old

That Nature was a white and mindless thing
Of perfect mathematical design
As snowflakes are, as blameless and as fine
(For lo, the stars grew gold and maddening).

Yes, there were horrors hinted in that night.
I thought a veil was parted from my eyes
And thought I saw our gods, of monstrous size,
Splash barefoot in our blood, and with delight.

MEDEA, HOMESICK

How many gifted witches, young and fair,
Have flunked, been ordinary, left the back-
Stooping study of their art, black
Or white, for love, that sudden foreigner?
Because chalk-fingered Wisdom streaks the hair,
Because the flame that flaps upon its wick
Rubrics the eye, I left behind the book
And washed my hands of ink, my homeland, my father.
But beauty doesn't travel well: the ocean,
Sun-strong years. The charms I knew by rote,
Irregular as verbs, decline to charm.
I cannot spell the simplest old potion
I learned for love. As for the antidote,
He discovered it himself, and is past harm.

THE WIFE OF THE MAN OF MANY WILES

Believe what you want to. Believe that I wove,
If you wish, twenty years, and waited, while you
Were knee-deep in blood, hip-deep in goddesses.

I've not much to show for twenty years' weaving—
I have but one half-finished cloth at the loom.
Perhaps it's the lengthy, meticulous grieving.

Explain how you want to. Believe I unravelled
At night what I stitched in the slow siesta,
How I kept them all waiting for me to finish,

The suitors, you call them. Believe what you want to.
Believe that they waited for me to finish,
Believe I beguiled them with nightly un-doings.

Believe what you want to. That they never touched me.
Believe your own stories, as you would have me do,
How you only survived by the wise infidelities.

Believe that each day you wrote me a letter
That never arrived. Kill all the damn suitors
If you think it will make you feel better.

ARIADNE AND THE REST

Maybe some Minoan Cinderella,
Sleeping Beauty or Snow White, concocted
To beguile the little girls indoors,
To keep them out of fights, discourage
Curiosity in swords, to keep them still
While nurses yanked out knots from tangled curls,
Maybe was some such didactic tale
Taught to all the small Minoan girls,
That such rewards there are for prettiness,
To show how being flustered can disarm.
If lips aren't red, why there is always paint,
And laces to make all the vital organs
Fit into a waist two hands can close
Around. Besides, to faint is feminine
And not, to men, without a certain charm.

Ariadne, more so than the rest,
Learned by rote the happy-ever-after,
Kept one eye peeled for princes, and ignored
Her cuckold father's horns, and all the laughter,
The rumors of her mother's wild affair,
The cellar where they kept deformity

Hungry in the dark beneath the stair.
Instead she watched for ships on the horizon,
The shroud-sailed ships that came with sacrifice.
When finally there was a prince on board,
She whispered in his sun-burnt ear, "At last!
Oh, free me from my labyrinthine days!
Oh, how each moment is so like the next,
Each leading to another just the same,
Each branching-off of time so like the rest,
A wearisome, well-ordered maze."

                       Better
Take her then, he thought, than have her spite
Raise up alarm. Besides, she saved my life.
And so the love set blackly into sail.
But when she sighed "forever" in her sleep,
And "happy ever after," and "the end,"
He suddenly recalled the dancing girls
In sweetly scented oils, the healthy slaves
With calloused hands, and in the palace softer
Servant maids, long linen pleated skirts,
The shepherd's white-armed, ox-eyed, swift-footed daughter.
"We shall stop here," he said, reaching an island.
Ariadne cooed, yes, yes, at every pause
As he gazed off at the knife-edge of the water.

But how the dawning emptied out the sky
Of stars, with an emptiness as clear
As ouzo and obscenely bright. She wailed.
All lost, suspended on that thread. Her mouth
Unhinged with disbelief—alone on Naxos
As the coward sailed. She wandered through
The puzzle of her hours, winding up
The filaments of dreams upon a spool.
The stars wheeled indolent upon their axis.
At noon the mirage of love shook everywhere.
The power of forgetfulness washed up
In amphorae along the shore—the god
Of wine himself spoke to her thirstiness:
"If your heart is empty, drink it full."
He pitied her and took her for his own,
He took her for his bride, although he was
Invisible, smelling of trampled grapes,
Sounding much like pebbles in the tide.

What it was she watched for on the sea
She forgot. No ships came for many years.
She was old when sailors took her home again.
They knew her name from myths, the hero-tales
Told to little boys—another princess
Jilted, drinking deep into the dregs

Of age. She could not tell them anything.
Her memory was like a broken toy.
She mumbled recipes, old rhymes, the song
Pasiphaë had sung while at the loom.
Sometimes halfway through a fairy tale,
She'd stop, announcing to the empty room,
"That's not it. The ending is all wrong."

TOUR OF THE LABYRINTH

And this is where they kept it, though their own,
Hungry in the dark beneath the stair,
And fed it apple cores, the odd soup bone,
And virgins with their torches of gold hair.

When howls were heard, they claimed it was the earth,
Subduction of a continental plate,
Put down their sherry glasses with thin mirth,
Excused themselves, and said that it was late.

But when the earth *did* make a mooing sound,
Stones that had been stacked into the wall
Knelt to the embracing of the ground.
Amid the gravity that struck them all

No one thought to go unlock the door.
Archaeologists, amazed to find
A skeleton they were not looking for,
Said it was the only of its kind.

They've unravelled the last days of the thing:
It lived a while on rats and bitumen,
And played with its one toy, a ball of string,
To puzzle out the darkness it was in.

AEAEA

Circe's Island

Less an island than a cry
Dumb animals might howl or sigh.

By dumb, I mean not, voicelessly,
But denote, "without syntax," free
From consonants' civility:

The "no hard feelings," the "goodbye,"
The (wh)y in you that is not I.

DAPHNE

Poet, Singer, Necromancer—
I cease to run. I halt you here,
Pursuer, with an answer:

Do what you will.
What blood you've set to music I
Can change to chlorophyll,

And root myself, and with my toes
Wind to subterranean streams.
Through solid rock my strength now grows.

Such now am I, I cease to eat,
But feed on flashes from your eyes;
Light, to my new cells, is meat.

Find then, when you seize my arm
That xylem thickens in my skin
And there are splinters in my charm.

I may give in; I do not lose.
Your hot stare cannot stop my shivering,
With delight, if I so choose.

ARACHNE GIVES THANKS TO ATHENA

It is no punishment. They are mistaken—
The brothers, the father. My prayers were answered.
I was all fingertips. Nothing was perfect:
What I had woven, the moths will have eaten;
At the end of my rope was a noose's knot.

Now it's no longer the thing, but the pattern,
And that will endure, even though webs be broken.

I, if not beautiful, am beauty's maker.
Old age cannot rob me, nor cowardly lovers.
The moon once pulled blood from me. Now I pull silver.
Here are the lines I pulled from my own belly—
Hang them with rainbows, ice, dewdrops, darkness.

TITHONUS

Do not look at me, and let me turn away
When you set me by the window in my chair,
Cover me with blankets, give me breakfast on a tray
(Soon the sky will glow with your red hair),

And I will convince us both that I am gone.
I will mutter nursery rhymes and drool,
Stare blankly as my bath is being drawn.
(You bathe my hollowed thighs. Your touch is cool.)

I will divert us with my nonsense words,
Forget your arms, the slight twitch of surprise
That I am light as paper, leaves, the egg-shell skulls of birds.
(My whole weight in the bulged spheres of my eyes.)

You feed me nectar from a spoon.
You bite your lip. I swallow and you wince.
(Once I too was beautiful.) Soon
You must go. You take my dish to rinse.

I watch as you tread, shining, up the hill,
I watch you as the world does, as I must.
(The landscape is anonymous, and still:
All elements, and minerals, and dust.)

VALE

I woke with longing from a dream of shoes
Snake-skin with leather soles and green as grass—
Tall, too-tight shoes that bit into my ankles
But walked over hearts like so much marble floor—
Marble veined & polished, the color of meat.
Then I beheld my bruised and naked feet,
The mark the snake strike made still on my ankle,
& I relived the last of my blue-sky moments—
A sudden sharpness in the blades of grass,
Venom mapping rivery veins to their source.
Your friend, red faced with lust and futile pursuit,
Stooped over where I had stumbled and understood,
Unlike you, he could not follow where I fled to.
The current dragging me down grew colder, stronger.
The sky ripened darkly as a plum
& I couldn't remember longing any longer.

The souls, in grey, carrying briefcases,
Glide iron escalators into the ground,
Great escalators many stories deep,
Each story stepping into the earth and silence,
Each soul reading the paper, turning the pages

Not looking back at the sun growing tarnished and small,
But adjusting their eyes to the buzz of fluorescent tubes.
They pay their tokens and line up along the platforms
Where trains approach and sigh and open their doors
And take them to cities of repetitive tasks.
Do you taste an electric bitterness of foil?
The dead have no pockets, must carry coins in their mouths,
Till everything, even saliva, tastes like money.

You crashed the witty soirée of little black dresses
And black tie. Too vivid, you sat at the grand piano
With its snaggle-toothed grimace of ebony and tusk
And tumbled black keys with white, unlocking your music.
Chromatics rainbowed from your fingertips.
The hostess turned & lifted her veil of dusk
And laughed like leaded crystal. The chandelier
Shuddered beneath its weight of faceted teardrops.
> Drifting down the river Liquor,
> Her blood no longer blood, but ichor,
> Sparkling up each one-way vein
> And down the artery again . . .
There was silence and an emptiness of glasses.
The wine that sobbed from the bottle's throat
Seemed red, till the last tune flew out the window
On its delicate bat-wings of semi-quavers.

Illuminated in tanks, the cave-fish swim
So tourists can peruse each skeleton
Stripped of the modesty of flesh, the scrim
Of skin, of blush, devoid of melanin.
This space between rocks is called Fat Man's Remorse,
Hold on to the railing over the Bottomless Pit,
This room looks like a Cathedral when it's lit,
Except without stained glass, or pews, or doors.
There is no elevator going up
Only an etiolated fire escape,
Long and twisted as a wayward weed
Germinated under rock. Do not look back,
They told you, don't look down, or fear will run
Through you like a vein of yellow metal,
Or subterranean stream, cold, mineral.
Even should you turn, what would you see?
That I am slowly gone invisible,
That love has made me see-through as a cave-fish,
The heart's shadow, tangled tube of gut,
Little bruises evolved in place of sight.

I had forgot how bottomless the night,
White-cold shone through the sky's moth-eaten blanket,
You held a lantern murderous to moths,
Which are for me the only butterflies,
You singed me with the tungsten of your eyes.

You whistled, *Memory will turn your head,*
With imitated voices or with silence.
Forever you will see someone slipping away.
And I fell for it all over again.

Helpless, as in some bureaucracy,
In a building that hummed like a drowsing machine
Although there was no sign of ventilation,
In a basement without windows, with plastic chairs,
And low walls with their fresh coats of grey paint,
A table with one antique magazine,
I went to the glaring counter and asked for you.
I said: I had done nothing, you'd done nothing.
They said, fill out this form. They said to wait.
They said that there was nothing they could do.

Hark, deep in their hives, the Dead are humming,
Dancing dizzy maps back to the flowers,
Storing up the honey of rue and thyme
In frail thesauruses of wax and paper,
In hexagons repeating like a rhyme.
Over the shimmering fields, the rest are coming.

I woke in the even measure of light and dark
We call evening, stumbled into the garden.
Sunflowers strained for one last glimpse of the sun.

Bumble bees were swinging their ball-bearing bodies
Between bright blossoms. Behold the spinster sisters,
Always humming, at their husbandry,
Hastening the summer to its harvest.

O slow and ceaseless weeping of the glass
That ripples windowpanes, O showers of dust
From life-bright skin that fall and blanket the floor,
O motes caught in the sunbeam's amber, O
Moon-round face and tidy hands of Time . . .

Now the dark is whistling to itself:
The train is climbing destiny's flat ladder,
The owl is putting her rhetorical question.

IV

FOR
THE
LOSERS
OF
THINGS

THE MISTAKE

The mistake was light and easy in my hand,
A seed meant to be borne upon the wind.
I did not have to bury it or throw,
Just open up my hand and let it go.

The mistake was dry and small and without weight,
A breeze quickly snatched it from my sight,
And even had I wanted to prevent,
Nobody could tell me where it went.

I did not think on the mistake again,
Until the spring came, soft, and full of rain,
And in the yard such dandelions grew
That bloomed and closed, and opened up, and blew.

THE TANTRUM

Struck with grief you were, though only four,
The day your mother cut her mermaid hair
And stood, a stranger, smiling at the door.

They frowned, tsk-tsked your willful, cruel despair,
When you slunk beneath the long piano strings
And sobbed until your lungs hiccupped for air,

Unbribable with curses, cake, playthings.
You mourned a mother now herself no more,
But brave and fashionable. The golden rings

That fringed her naked neck, whom were they for?
Not you, but for the world, now in your place,
A full eclipse. You wept down on the floor;

She wept up in her room. They told you this:
That she could grow it back, and just as long,
They told you, lying always about loss,

For you know she never did. And they were wrong.

FISHING

The two of them stood in the middle water,
The current slipping away, quick and cold,
The sun slow at his zenith, sweating gold,
Once, in some sullen summer of father and daughter.
Maybe he regretted he had brought her—
She'd rather have been elsewhere, her look told—
Perhaps a year ago, but now too old.
Still, she remembered lessons he had taught her:
To cast towards shadows, where the sunlight fails
And fishes shelter in the undergrowth.
And when the unseen strikes, how all else pales
Beside the bright-dark struggle, the rainbow wroth,
Life and death weighed in the shining scales,
The invisible line pulled taut that links them both.

THE POET'S DREAM OF
HERSELF AS A YOUNG GIRL

How talented, my daughter,
In all media of art—
Oils, charcoal, water,
The rending of the heart.

They told you you were clever,
But the heart is not an egg
That breaks once and forever;
It's a dog that learns to beg

For bones dropped on the floor,
To lick up spilt milk there
Curdled with tears, to adore
From the shelter under a chair.

You thought that you were wise,
But the brain is not a box
Inlaid with galaxies;
It's the steel trap and the fox

Gnawing its foot to escape
While buzzards dial the sky
And you see the huntsman's cape
Crimson as liberty.

For your sake, I still loathe
The way he made you trip
On the long sleeve of your love,
Your innocence let slip

Like a bra-strap over your shoulder.
But you already know the rest:
How you died, then got older,
How you buried your heart in my chest.

THE SCHOOL OF DREAMS

It is an afternoon
With chalk dust in the light.
The dusk is coming soon
And the answer is not right.

The answer is not right
And the bell is going to ring,
And red ink, like a blight,
Has tainted everything:

The leaves upon the trees,
The leaves that fall and rest,
The light, that by degrees,
Is failing in the west,

Everything will burn
With a shade of shame,
Because it is your turn,
Because you hear your name,

And cannot solve for y.
Minutes go to waste,
The slate blank as a sky,
Imperfectly erased.

The bell is going to chime.
There's nothing you can do
But to flip a dime
Between false and true.

The problem still remains,
It isn't what you think.
Failure's in your veins,
Red as any ink.

STUDY IN WHITE

A friend, an artist, phoned me up and said,
What shall I do for flesh? And what for bone?
All has some white, and the best white is lead.

But lead gets in the flesh and in the bone,
And if you are a woman, in the child
You bear years hence, and I know, have read

That you may use titanium or zinc,
Not poisonous, but you may be reviled
Because you lack the seriousness bred

For art in men—or how else could you think
Of compromise in this. And I own
I've tried them both, but the best white is lead

For making up the colors bold and mild,
Conceiving still lifes, matching tone with tone
To reproduce the spectra of the dead.

And I have stood for hours at the sink
Scrubbing white from hands until they bled.
And still my hands are stained, and still I think—
O flesh and blood—but the best white is lead.

ON VIEWING AN EXHIBIT OF PAINTINGS,
THE TREASURES OF VENICE

In certain old Venetian paintings, just
The hard, expensive things look real, and shine:
The pearls upon some lady's dim, grey bust,
The goblet, gold, enriched with sanguine wine.

The dagger glows, but not the bloodless hand,
The ivory of teeth, but not the lips,
The silver hourglass, but not the sand
That drains away. The artists' fingertips

Let slip all warmth, all flesh, as through a sieve.
Beneath sly eyelids, shadowed by fine lashes,
Like coins half-hidden in a folded sleeve,
The counterfeit of eyes furtively flashes.

THE MACHINES MOURN
THE PASSING OF PEOPLE

We miss the warmth of their clumsy hands,
The oil of their fingers, the cleansing of use
That warded off dust, and the warm abuse
Lavished upon us as reprimands.

We were kicked like dogs when we were broken,
But we did not whimper. We gritted our cogs—
An honor it was to be treated as dogs,
To incur such warm words roughly spoken,

The way that they pleaded with us if we balked—
"Come on, come on" in a hoarse whisper
As they would urge a reluctant lover—
The feel of their warm breath when they talked!

How could we guess they would ever be gone?
We are shorn now of tasks, and the lovely work—
Not toiling, not spinning—like lilies that shirk—
Like the brash dandelions that savage the lawn.

The air now is silent of curses or praise.
Jilted, abandoned to hells of what weather,
Left to our own devices forever,
We watch the sun rust at the end of its days.

MENIELLE

I've dragged my weary feet home after dusk
And a day of boiling tea and burning milk.
Long have I toiled at the thankless task.

I've done the washing up, smiled through my mask,
Taken dictation and jobs of that ilk
And dragged my weary feet home after dusk.

Some give orders who could simply ask
In voices hissing soft as rustled silk.
Long have I toiled at the thankless task

And long have I made change, and made it brisk,
Though nothing changes: customers carp and bilk,
& I drag my weary feet home after dusk.

To soothe the angry, I have tapped the cask
Of patience dry, and nursed them through their sulk.
Long have I toiled at the thankless task

And wished I could glare like a basilisk
Or Medusa, but I'm the one who turns to chalk,
Dragging my stony feet home after dusk.
Long have I toiled at the thankless task.

WATCHING THE NEWS
AFTER THE TORNADOES

"It's like," decides the telecaster,
"A movie set of . . . some disaster,"
Lacking, in the wake of these
Tornadoes, useful similes.

But metaphor's the thing that carries
Cold front into warm, that buries
Metal in a man's deep chest,
Uncorks an oak tree with a twist.

The metaphor is green with power,
Spins a hundred miles an hour,
And with a sound of trains it blows
Apart all windows as it goes.

THE MAN WHO WOULDN'T
PLANT WILLOW TREES

Willows are messy trees. Hair in their eyes,
They weep like women after too much wine
And not enough love. They litter a lawn with leaves
Like the butts of regrets smoked down to the filter.

They are always out of kilter. Thirsty as drunks,
They'll sink into a sewer with their roots.
They have no pride. There's never enough sorrow.
A breeze threatens and they shake with sobs.

Willows are slobs, and must be cleaned up after.
They'll bust up pipes just looking for a drink.
Their fingers tremble, but make wicked switches.
They claim they are sorry, but they whisper it.

MOVING SALE

How came we by this quantity of junk?
A kind of shipwreck, washed up in the yard,
Glittering cheaply in the sun: the marred,
The obsolete, redundant. We are sunk
Deep in things. That hermit crab, the soul,
Crawled up tight into its borrowed shell,
Grows attached to where it has to dwell.
The world is furnished with the physical.
But one by one, the strangers lift away
What we have touched and worn, to curse and bless
Our things to a new life of usefulness,
And we, the sunlight spent, call it a day,
And rising up at last, feel rich and strange.
It is the weight and weightlessness of change.

WHERE WE MOVED TO

on the occasion of our new address

I sweep and you find fault with sweeping:
I have failed corners. Dust remains.
But in your cup the tea is steeping,
The train shudders the windowpanes.
The tea is steeping, sending up
Its steam, leaking its amber ink
Into the crazing of the cup.
So much dust. It makes me think
How the skin cells softly rain,
Invisibly, upon the floor
Which we shall have to sweep again.
I cough. We're so close to the tracks
Both sides are wrong. The window glass
So old it ripples. All is flux.
Windows trickle like molasses.
The train, pacing to and fro,
Rails against its ties, a bore,
But like a river, it must go
Along the path it went before.
The liquor of your tea grows cold

Before you drink it. How erratic
The motes sway in the rippled gold
To the radio's sweet static.
I am almost done with sweeping.
You nod, even though dust remains.
The cough returns. The clock is keeping
Time to the keening of the trains.
The last broom stroke—the dust balls bustle.
I take my breath in jagged sherds.
And in my lungs I hear a rustle
Like a shuffling of cards,
A fortune-teller at her Tarot
Telling the future: dust tomorrow.

AIRING

Each partner has a task, and this is mine:
That there is always something on the line.
The laundry dances in its emptiness.
The shoulders shrug, the sleeves reach to caress . . .

The wind is pacing through the upper floors,
Opening and slamming all the doors,
Like an argument in married love
Repetition will not cure it of.

There is a kind of vacancy that hurts.
The wind is trying on the white of shirts.
I open up the door. As for a hug,
The sleeves blow out to me. The shoulders shrug.

In its emptiness, the laundry dances.
The wind's all empty threats and second chances.
The door slams shut. The white bed sheets tender
A sort of peace, the terms of their surrender.

FOR THE LOSERS OF THINGS

She is shedding belongings wherever she goes—
Necklaces, combs, virginity, lovers,
Bus-money, phone numbers, gifts and their givers,
In the laundry, perhaps, in the pockets of clothes,

Dropped in the aisle of the east-bound train,
Slipped down the seat of her car-pool-ride
(Or her eighteenth year, in the Lenten-tide),
And places more difficult to explain,

Like deep-in-dreams, like half-way-there . . .
She has left by her unfinished drink at the bar
The keys to her house and the keys to her car,
The ribbon that orders her unruly hair . . .

He is calling her number; she is not in—
She is shedding her dress, like scales, like love,
A dry, silk hide she has cast off—
She is ranging abroad in her new skin.

THE POET'S SISTER

for Jocelyn

The poet's sister lives the poet's life:
She keeps all her belongings in her car,
Then leaves the car behind. It is enough:
A whim's the wind that blows the compass-star.

The poet's sister drives with any friend
Pushing west, or any westering love,
Sun-sets her gaze over the pulling horizon,
Takes any job that pays less than enough

To keep her there; she busses dirty dishes,
Rises to waitressing, likes living rough,
Resides in tents and bathes among the fishes.
There is no roof that's clear or high enough.

The poet's sister buys just one-way tickets,
Leaves no address to forward winter stuff.
She's seen the blast-off of Space Shuttle rockets;
She knows that gravity is not enough

To hold us down, that it is no excuse.
The poet's sister has come close to death,
Had blood combed from her hair, been dreadful news
At an hour when shrieking phones are dread enough,

Been stitched and splinted. If the poet's bones
Don't twinge, foretelling snow, and if her love
Dawns steady from the east, and if she owns
Health-benefits, a cat, too much to leave

Or cut her losses with a pocket knife
That chains her to her keys and carefulness:
The poet's sister lives, which is enough
Of loose rope-bridges and the sky's abyss.

ELEGY FOR THE LOST UMBRELLA

To lose an umbrella is nothing. But to lose
An umbrella you've held on to year after year
Through various chances of rain, that you've gone back for
Into restaurants and shops, with your sopping shoes,
And leaning against the wall like a confident lover,
There it was—*You'd be back.* Beautiful!
Sage green, sprinkled with flowers, the cloth-covered
    handle . . .
But left on a west-bound train—everything's over
Like the end of a movie. You are suddenly light
As if it were that hook that was holding you steady
Through shifting sands of years, always ready
With its shadow and kindly cane. Or it might
Be you feel dizzy because of the sudden flare
Of Possible Umbrellas opening all around—
The ones you may yet have, flimsy or sound,
But fickle, tugging you off into thin air.

WHY REASON CAN'T OVERCOME
AN IRRATIONAL FEAR

The phobia whispers to me that I am special,
His chosen, fondly dishevelling my nerves with his fingers.
Statistics, he scoffs, are for those without destinies,
Who are less safe in cars, more likely hit by lightning
Than to plummet out of the sky in an aeroplane.
Logic, seducing with cool, promiscuous numbers,
Will exchange me for another. But dread will not leave me.

We are soulmates, he says, and in another death
We invented flight. Remember the sun on our backs,
The feathers loosening from the sticky wax
When the heavens disowned us like two meteors
And we shattered the flat mirror of the ocean?

Most thoughtful of bridegrooms, on our honeymoon
He holds my fidgety heart as our flight takes off
And I weep for love of everyone on the plane,
For the earth, a robin's egg in a porcelain cup,
Because none of them knows they are doomed should I fall
    asleep,
Blink my dry vigilance, get cozy with hope,
That only the force of my fear is lifting us up.

NIGHT SHIFT

Two a.m. The freight train files its grievance
Into the tall cabinet of the night.
Beyond the street lamps, stars grow recondite.
The insomniac is listening to distance
Shifting register, a kind of sorrow.
The train is keening in concatenations,
It is too late. It's already tomorrow—
Even when nothing happens, time is ever
Ticking down the track between two stations.
The hours are numbered, and then they elide.
The sick child is tossing in her fever,
The bridegroom turns him from the bride.
The insomniac turns the cool, white page. The lover
Turns the pillow to the cooler side.